This

# Manifest That Shxt Journal

belongs to:

_____

_____

_____

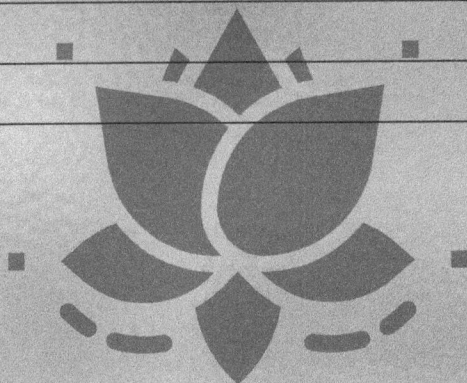

" We All Want Success, Love, Wealth and Happiness. But Are We...... Manifesting That Shxt?."

Shavon Parker

# Morning Routine

Date: _____

## Today's Positive Affirmation

|  |
|--|
|  |

## Today's Personal Goal

(Write down what you want to achieve for yourself today.)

_____

_____

## Today's Intention

(Write down how you want this day to be.)

|  |
|--|
|  |

## 5 Things I am grateful for

#1 _____
#2 _____
#3 _____
#4 _____
#5 _____

## Today I Manifest....

(Notice five things that you can see and write them down.)

| #1 |
|----|
| #2 |
| #3 |
| #4 |
| #5 |

# Evening Routine

## This went well today

## 5 Things I am proud of

#1 
#2 
#3 
#4 
#5 

## This made me feel happy

## My thoughts about today

# Morning Routine

Date: _____

## Today's Positive Affirmation

```
┌─────────────────────────────────────────────────────────────┐
│                                                             │
│                                                             │
│                                                             │
│                                                             │
└─────────────────────────────────────────────────────────────┘
```

## Today's Personal Goal

(Write down what you want to achieve for yourself today.)

_____

_____

## Today's Intention

(Write down how you want this day to be.)

```
┌─────────────────────────────────────────────────────────────┐
│                                                             │
│                                                             │
│                                                             │
└─────────────────────────────────────────────────────────────┘
```

## 5 Things I am grateful for

#1 _____

#2 _____

#3 _____

#4 _____

#5 _____

## Today I Manifest.....

(Notice five things that you can see and write them down.)

#1 _____

#2 _____

#3 _____

#4 _____

#5 _____

# Evening Routine

## This went well today

## 5 Things I am proud of

#1

#2

#3

#4

#5

## This made me feel happy

## My thoughts about today

# Morning Routine

Date: _____

## Today's Positive Affirmation

```
┌─────────────────────────────────────────────────────────────┐
│                                                             │
│                                                             │
│                                                             │
│                                                             │
└─────────────────────────────────────────────────────────────┘
```

## Today's Personal Goal
(Write down what you want to achieve for yourself today.)

_____

_____

## Today's Intention
(Write down how you want this day to be.)

```
┌─────────────────────────────────────────────────────────────┐
│                                                             │
│                                                             │
│                                                             │
│                                                             │
└─────────────────────────────────────────────────────────────┘
```

## 5 Things I am grateful for

#1 _____

#2 _____

#3 _____

#4 _____

#5 _____

## Today I Manifest....
(Notice five things that you can see and write them down.)

#1 _____

#2 _____

#3 _____

#4 _____

#5 _____

# Evening Routine

### This went well today

### 5 Things I am proud of

#1

#2

#3

#4

#5

### This made me feel happy

### My thoughts about today

# Morning Routine

Date: _____

## Today's Positive Affirmation

<br>
<br>
<br>
<br>

## Today's Personal Goal

(Write down what you want to achieve for yourself today.)

_____

_____

## Today's Intention

(Write down how you want this day to be.)

<br>
<br>
<br>
<br>

## 5 Things I am grateful for

#1 _____

#2 _____

#3 _____

#4 _____

#5 _____

## Today I Mannifest....

(Notice five things that you can see and write them down.)

| #1 | |
|----|----|
| #2 | |
| #3 | |
| #4 | |
| #5 | |

# Evening Routine

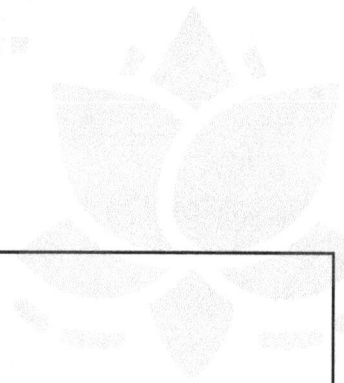

## This went well today

## 5 Things I am proud of

#1

#2

#3

#4

#5

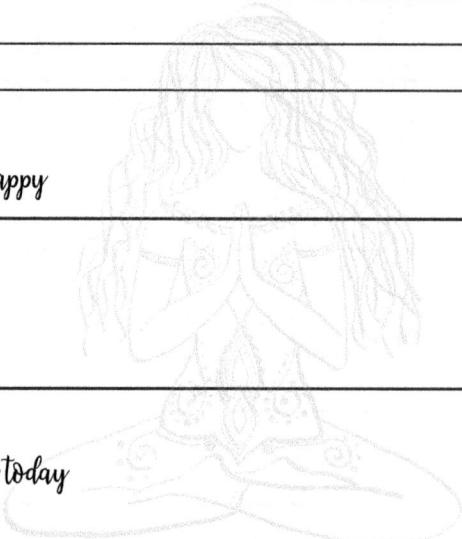

## This made me feel happy

## My thoughts about today

Revive Your **Light**!
Manifest Your **Dreams**!
Realize Your **Worth**!

# Morning Routine

Date: _____

## Today's Positive Affirmation

```
[                                                          ]
```

## Today's Personal Goal

(Write down what you want to achieve for yourself today.)

_____

_____

## Today's Intention

(Write down how you want this day to be.)

```
[                                                          ]
```

## 5 Things I am grateful for

| | |
|---|---|
| #1 | |
| #2 | |
| #3 | |
| #4 | |
| #5 | |

## Today I Manifest....

(Notice five things that you can see and write them down.)

| | |
|---|---|
| #1 | |
| #2 | |
| #3 | |
| #4 | |
| #5 | |

# Evening Routine

## This went well today

## 5 Things I am proud of

#1

#2

#3

#4

#5

## This made me feel happy

## My Thoughts about today

Shout To The Universe
"All Good Things Come To Me"
Watch Your Manifestations
Become A Reality.

# Morning Routine

Date: _____

## Today's Positive Affirmation

```



```

## Today's Personal Goal    (Write down what you want to achieve for yourself today.)

_____

_____

## Today's Intention    (Write down how you want this day to be.)

```



```

## 5 Things I am grateful for

#1 _____
#2 _____
#3 _____
#4 _____
#5 _____

## Today I Manifest....    (Notice five things that you can see and write them down.)

| | |
|---|---|
| #1 | |
| #2 | |
| #3 | |
| #4 | |
| #5 | |

# Evening Routine

## This went well today

## 5 Things I am proud of

#1

#2

#3

#4

#5

## This made me feel happy

## My thoughts about today

# Morning Routine

Date: _____

## Today's Positive Affirmation

┌─────────────────────────────────────────────────────────┐
│                                                         │
│                                                         │
│                                                         │
│                                                         │
└─────────────────────────────────────────────────────────┘

## Today's Personal Goal

(Write down what you want to achieve for yourself today.)

_____

_____

## Today's Intention

(Write down how you want this day to be.)

┌─────────────────────────────────────────────────────────┐
│                                                         │
│                                                         │
│                                                         │
└─────────────────────────────────────────────────────────┘

## 5 Things I am grateful for

#1 _____

#2 _____

#3 _____

#4 _____

#5 _____

## Today I Manifest....

(Notice five things that you can see and write them down.)

| #1 | |
|----|--|
| #2 | |
| #3 | |
| #4 | |
| #5 | |

# Evening Routine

### This went well today

### 5 Things I am proud of

#1

#2

#3

#4

#5

### This made me feel happy

### My thoughts about today

# Morning Routine

Date: _____

## Today's Positive Affirmation

```
[blank box]
```

## Today's Personal Goal

(Write down what you want to achieve for yourself today.)

_____

_____

## Today's Intention

(Write down how you want this day to be.)

```
[blank box]
```

## 5 Things I am grateful for

#1 _____
#2 _____
#3 _____
#4 _____
#5 _____

## Today I Manifest.....

(Notice five things that you can see and write them down.)

| | |
|---|---|
| #1 | |
| #2 | |
| #3 | |
| #4 | |
| #5 | |

# Evening Routine

## This went well today

## 5 Things I am proud of

#1 _____
#2 _____
#3 _____
#4 _____
#5 _____

## This made me feel happy

## My thoughts about today

_____
_____
_____
_____
_____
_____
_____
_____
_____
_____

Manifest The Things
you Want,
By Believing In Their
Existence

# Morning Routine

Date: _____

## Today's Positive Affirmation

<br>

## Today's Personal Goal

(Write down what you want to achieve for yourself today.)

_____

_____

## Today's Intention

(Write down how you want this day to be.)

<br>

## 5 Things I am grateful for

#1 _____
#2 _____
#3 _____
#4 _____
#5 _____

## Today I Manifest....

(Notice five things that you can see and write them down.)

#1 _____
#2 _____
#3 _____
#4 _____
#5 _____

# Evening Routine

## This went well today

## 5 Things I am proud of

#1 _____

#2 _____

#3 _____

#4 _____

#5 _____

## This made me feel happy

## My thoughts about today

_____

_____

_____

_____

_____

_____

_____

_____

_____

_____

_____

# Morning Routine

Date: _____

## Today's Positive Affirmation

```
[                                                              ]
```

## Today's Personal Goal

(Write down what you want to achieve for yourself today.)

_____

_____

## Today's Intention

(Write down how you want this day to be.)

```
[                                                              ]
```

## 5 Things I am grateful for

#1 _____

#2 _____

#3 _____

#4 _____

#5 _____

## Today I Manifest.....

(Notice five things that you can see and write them down.)

| | |
|---|---|
| #1 | |
| #2 | |
| #3 | |
| #4 | |
| #5 | |

# Evening Routine

This went well today

5 Things I am proud of

#1

#2

#3

#4

#5

This made me feel happy

My thoughts about today

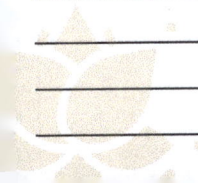

# Morning Routine

Date: _____

## Today's Positive Affirmation

```
┌──────────────────────────────────────────────────────────┐
│                                                          │
│                                                          │
│                                                          │
│                                                          │
└──────────────────────────────────────────────────────────┘
```

## Today's Personal Goal

(Write down what you want to achieve for yourself today.)

_____

_____

## Today's Intention

(Write down how you want this day to be.)

```
┌──────────────────────────────────────────────────────────┐
│                                                          │
│                                                          │
│                                                          │
│                                                          │
└──────────────────────────────────────────────────────────┘
```

## 5 Things I am grateful for

#1 _____

#2 _____

#3 _____

#4 _____

#5 _____

## Today I Manifest....

(Notice five things that you can see and write them down.)

#1 _____

#2 _____

#3 _____

#4 _____

#5 _____

# Evening Routine

## This went well today

## 5 Things I am proud of

#1

#2

#3

#4

#5

## This made me feel happy

## My thoughts about today

# Morning Routine

Date: _____

## Today's Positive Affirmation

|  |
|---|
|  |

## Today's Personal Goal

(Write down what you want to achieve for yourself today.)

_____

_____

## Today's Intention

(Write down how you want this day to be.)

|  |
|---|
|  |

## 5 Things I am grateful for

#1 _____
#2 _____
#3 _____
#4 _____
#5 _____

## Today I Manifest....

(Notice five things that you can see and write them down.)

| #1 |
|---|
| #2 |
| #3 |
| #4 |
| #5 |

# Evening Routine

### This went well today

### 5 Things I am proud of

#1 _____

#2 _____

#3 _____

#4 _____

#5 _____

### This made me feel happy

### My thoughts about today

# Morning Routine

Date: _____

## Today's Positive Affirmation

```
[                                                        ]
```

## Today's Personal Goal

(Write down what you want to achieve for yourself today.)

_____

_____

## Today's Intention

(Write down how you want this day to be.)

```
[                                                        ]
```

## 5 Things I am grateful for

#1 _____

#2 _____

#3 _____

#4 _____

#5 _____

## Today I Manifest....

(Notice five things that you can see and write them down.)

| | |
|---|---|
| #1 | |
| #2 | |
| #3 | |
| #4 | |
| #5 | |

# Evening Routine

## This went well today

## 5 Things I am proud of

#1

#2

#3

#4

#5

## This made me feel happy

## My thoughts about today

"To live your greatest life, you must first become a leader within yourself. Take charge of your life, begin attracting and MANIFESTING all that you desire in life." – Sonia Ricotti

# Morning Routine

Date: _____

## Today's Positive Affirmation

---

## Today's Personal Goal

(Write down what you want to achieve for yourself today.)

_____

_____

## Today's Intention

(Write down how you want this day to be.)

---

## 5 Things I am grateful for

#1 _____

#2 _____

#3 _____

#4 _____

#5 _____

## Today I Manifest....

(Notice five things that you can see and write them down.)

| | |
|---|---|
| #1 | |
| #2 | |
| #3 | |
| #4 | |
| #5 | |

# Evening Routine

This went well today

| |
|---|
| |

5 Things I am proud of

#1 _____
#2 _____
#3 _____
#4 _____
#5 _____

This made me feel happy

| |
|---|
| |

My thoughts about today

_____
_____
_____
_____
_____
_____
_____
_____
_____
_____
_____

# Morning Routine

Date: _____

## Today's Positive Affirmation

```
┌─────────────────────────────────────────────┐
│                                             │
│                                             │
│                                             │
│                                             │
└─────────────────────────────────────────────┘
```

## Today's Personal Goal

(Write down what you want to achieve for yourself today.)

_____

_____

## Today's Intention

(Write down how you want this day to be.)

```
┌─────────────────────────────────────────────┐
│                                             │
│                                             │
│                                             │
│                                             │
└─────────────────────────────────────────────┘
```

## 5 Things I am grateful for

#1 _____

#2 _____

#3 _____

#4 _____

#5 _____

## Today I Manifest....

(Notice five things that you can see and write them down.)

| #1 | |
|----|--|
| #2 | |
| #3 | |
| #4 | |
| #5 | |

# Evening Routine

This went well today

5 Things I am proud of

#1

#2

#3

#4

#5

This made me feel happy

My thoughts about today

"I attract into my life whatever I give my attention, energy, and focus to, whether positive or negative."

- Michael Losier

# Morning Routine

Date: _____

## Today's Positive Affirmation

[ ]

## Today's Personal Goal  (Write down what you want to achieve for yourself today.)

_____

_____

## Today's Intention  (Write down how you want this day to be.)

[ ]

## 5 Things I am grateful for

#1 _____
#2 _____
#3 _____
#4 _____
#5 _____

## Today I Manifest....  (Notice five things that you can see and write them down.)

| #1 | |
|----|--|
| #2 | |
| #3 | |
| #4 | |
| #5 | |

# Evening Routine

This went well today

5 Things I am proud of

#1

#2

#3

#4

#5

This made me feel happy

My thoughts about today

# Morning Routine

Date: _____

## Today's Positive Affirmation

<br><br><br><br><br>

## Today's Personal Goal

(Write down what you want to achieve for yourself today.)

_____

_____

## Today's Intention

(Write down how you want this day to be.)

<br><br><br><br>

## 5 Things I am grateful for

#1 _____

#2 _____

#3 _____

#4 _____

#5 _____

## Today I Manifest....

(Notice five things that you can see and write them down.)

| | |
|---|---|
| #1 | |
| #2 | |
| #3 | |
| #4 | |
| #5 | |

# Evening Routine

## This went well today

## 5 Things I am proud of

#1

#2

#3

#4

#5

## This made me feel happy

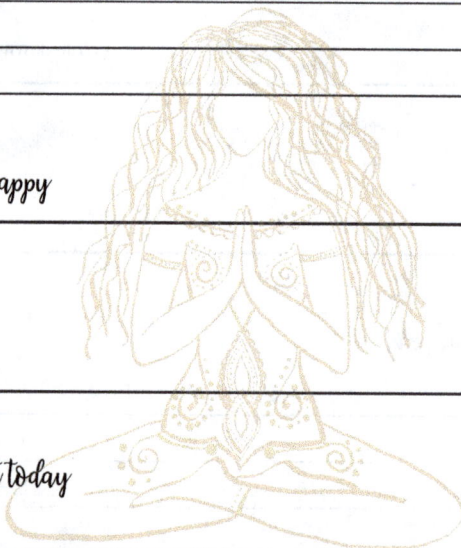

## My thoughts about today

Date: _____

# Today I Manifest Money!

I Am A Money Magnet
Money Comes To Me Easily,
Frequently and Abundantly

(Repeat Below)

| #1 | |
|----|--|
| #2 | |
| #3 | |
| #4 | |
| #5 | |

| #1 | |
|----|--|
| #2 | |
| #3 | |
| #4 | |
| #5 | |

| #1 | |
|----|--|
| #2 | |
| #3 | |
| #4 | |
| #5 | |

# Morning Routine

Date: _____

## Today's Positive Affirmation

```
[                                                                    ]
```

## Today's Personal Goal

(Write down what you want to achieve for yourself today.)

_____

_____

## Today's Intention

(Write down how you want this day to be.)

```
[                                                                    ]
```

## 5 Things I am grateful for

#1 _____
#2 _____
#3 _____
#4 _____
#5 _____

## Today I Manifest....

(Notice five things that you can see and write them down.)

#1 _____
#2 _____
#3 _____
#4 _____
#5 _____

# Evening Routine

This went well today

_(blank box)_

5 Things I am proud of

#1 _____
#2 _____
#3 _____
#4 _____
#5 _____

This made me feel happy

_(blank box)_

My thoughts about today

_____
_____
_____
_____
_____
_____
_____
_____
_____
_____

# Morning Routine

Date: _____

## Today's Positive Affirmation

```
┌─────────────────────────────────────────────┐
│                                             │
│                                             │
│                                             │
└─────────────────────────────────────────────┘
```

## Today's Personal Goal

(Write down what you want to achieve for yourself today.)

_____

_____

## Today's Intention

(Write down how you want this day to be.)

```
┌─────────────────────────────────────────────┐
│                                             │
│                                             │
│                                             │
└─────────────────────────────────────────────┘
```

## 5 Things I am grateful for

#1 _____

#2 _____

#3 _____

#4 _____

#5 _____

## Today I Manifest....

(Notice five things that you can see and write them down.)

| | |
|---|---|
| #1 | |
| #2 | |
| #3 | |
| #4 | |
| #5 | |

# Evening Routine

## This went well today

## 5 Things I am proud of

#1

#2

#3

#4

#5

## This made me feel happy

## My thoughts about today

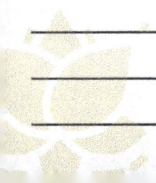

Date: _____

# Today I Manifest Love!

I Am Love, I Am Open To Receiving
Love From Everyone Around Me, I
Am Capable Of Love

(Repeat Below)

#1 _____
#2 _____
#3 _____
#4 _____
#5 _____

#1 _____
#2 _____
#3 _____
#4 _____
#5 _____

#1 _____
#2 _____
#3 _____
#4 _____
#5 _____

# Morning Routine

Date: _____

## Today's Positive Affirmation

```

```

## Today's Personal Goal
(Write down what you want to achieve for yourself today.)

_____

_____

## Today's Intention
(Write down how you want this day to be.)

```

```

## 5 Things I am grateful for

#1 _____
#2 _____
#3 _____
#4 _____
#5 _____

## Today I Manifest....
(Notice five things that you can see and write them down.)

| | |
|---|---|
| #1 | |
| #2 | |
| #3 | |
| #4 | |
| #5 | |

# Evening Routine

This went well today

5 Things I am proud of

#1

#2

#3

#4

#5

This made me feel happy

My thoughts about today

# Morning Routine

Date: _____

## Today's Positive Affirmation

```
┌─────────────────────────────────────────────────┐
│                                                 │
│                                                 │
│                                                 │
│                                                 │
└─────────────────────────────────────────────────┘
```

## Today's Personal Goal

(Write down what you want to achieve for yourself today.)

_____

_____

## Today's Intention

(Write down how you want this day to be.)

```
┌─────────────────────────────────────────────────┐
│                                                 │
│                                                 │
│                                                 │
│                                                 │
└─────────────────────────────────────────────────┘
```

## 5 Things I am grateful for

#1 _____

#2 _____

#3 _____

#4 _____

#5 _____

## Today I Manifest....

(Notice five things that you can see and write them down.)

| | |
|---|---|
| #1 | |
| #2 | |
| #3 | |
| #4 | |
| #5 | |

# Evening Routine

## This went well today

## 5 Things I am proud of

#1 _____

#2 _____

#3 _____

#4 _____

#5 _____

## This made me feel happy

## My thoughts about today

_____

_____

_____

_____

_____

_____

_____

_____

_____

_____

_____

# Morning Routine

Date: _____

## Today's Positive Affirmation

```
┌─────────────────────────────────────────────────────────────┐
│                                                             │
│                                                             │
│                                                             │
│                                                             │
└─────────────────────────────────────────────────────────────┘
```

## Today's Personal Goal

(Write down what you want to achieve for yourself today.)

_____

_____

## Today's Intention

(Write down how you want this day to be.)

```
┌─────────────────────────────────────────────────────────────┐
│                                                             │
│                                                             │
│                                                             │
└─────────────────────────────────────────────────────────────┘
```

## 5 Things I am grateful for

#1 _____

#2 _____

#3 _____

#4 _____

#5 _____

## Today I Manifest....

(Notice five things that you can see and write them down.)

| #1 | |
|----|----|
| #2 | |
| #3 | |
| #4 | |
| #5 | |

# Evening Routine

## This went well today

## 5 Things I am proud of

#1

#2

#3

#4

#5

## This made me feel happy

## My thoughts about today

I am
Fearless

I am
Strong

I am
Beautiful

I am
LOVE

I am
Brave

# Morning Routine

Date: _____

## Today's Positive Affirmation

```
[                                                                    ]
```

## Today's Personal Goal

(Write down what you want to achieve for yourself today.)

_____

_____

## Today's Intention

(Write down how you want this day to be.)

```
[                                                                    ]
```

## 5 Things I am grateful for

#1 _____

#2 _____

#3 _____

#4 _____

#5 _____

## Today I Manifest....

(Notice five things that you can see and write them down.)

#1 _____

#2 _____

#3 _____

#4 _____

#5 _____

# Evening Routine

This went well today

5 Things I am proud of

#1 _____

#2 _____

#3 _____

#4 _____

#5 _____

This made me feel happy

My thoughts about today

_____

_____

_____

_____

_____

_____

_____

_____

_____

_____

_____

# Morning Routine

Date: _____

## Today's Positive Affirmation

```

```

## Today's Personal Goal          (Write down what you want to achieve for yourself today.)

_____

_____

## Today's Intention          (Write down how you want this day to be.)

```

```

## 5 Things I am grateful for

#1 _____
#2 _____
#3 _____
#4 _____
#5 _____

## Today I Manifest....          (Notice five things that you can see and write them down.)

| #1 | |
|----|--|
| #2 | |
| #3 | |
| #4 | |
| #5 | |

# Evening Routine

This went well today

5 Things I am proud of

#1

#2

#3

#4

#5

This made me feel happy

My thoughts about today

# Morning Routine

Date: _____

## Today's Positive Affirmation

```
[                                                              ]
```

## Today's Personal Goal

(Write down what you want to achieve for yourself today.)

_____

_____

## Today's Intention

(Write down how you want this day to be.)

```
[                                                              ]
```

## 5 Things I am grateful for

| | |
|---|---|
| #1 | |
| #2 | |
| #3 | |
| #4 | |
| #5 | |

## Today I Manifest....

(Notice five things that you can see and write them down.)

| | |
|---|---|
| #1 | |
| #2 | |
| #3 | |
| #4 | |
| #5 | |

# Evening Routine

This went well today

[ ]

5 Things I am proud of

#1 _____

#2 _____

#3 _____

#4 _____

#5 _____

This made me feel happy

[ ]

My thoughts about today

_____

_____

_____

_____

_____

_____

_____

_____

_____

_____

"It's Already Yours."

~The Universe

# Morning Routine

Date: _____

## Today's Positive Affirmation

[ ]

## Today's Personal Goal

(Write down what you want to achieve for yourself today.)

_____
_____

## Today's Intention

(Write down how you want this day to be.)

[ ]

## 5 Things I am grateful for

#1 _____
#2 _____
#3 _____
#4 _____
#5 _____

## Today I Manifest....

(Notice five things that you can see and write them down.)

| #1 | |
|----|----|
| #2 | |
| #3 | |
| #4 | |
| #5 | |

# Evening Routine

## This went well today

## 5 Things I am proud of

#1
#2
#3
#4
#5

## This made me feel happy

## My thoughts about today

# Morning Routine

Date: _____

## Today's Positive Affirmation

_____

## Today's Personal Goal

(Write down what you want to achieve for yourself today.)

_____

_____

## Today's Intention

(Write down how you want this day to be.)

_____

## 5 Things I am grateful for

#1 _____

#2 _____

#3 _____

#4 _____

#5 _____

## Today I Manifest...

(Notice five things that you can see and write them down.)

| #1 | |
| #2 | |
| #3 | |
| #4 | |
| #5 | |

# Evening Routine

## This went well today

---

## 5 Things I am proud of

#1 _____

#2 _____

#3 _____

#4 _____

#5 _____

## This made me feel happy

---

## My thoughts about today

_____

_____

_____

_____

_____

_____

_____

_____

_____

# Morning Routine

Date: _____

## Today's Positive Affirmation

<br><br><br>

## Today's Personal Goal

(Write down what you want to achieve for yourself today.)

_____

_____

## Today's Intention

(Write down how you want this day to be.)

<br><br><br>

## 5 Things I am grateful for

#1 _____

#2 _____

#3 _____

#4 _____

#5 _____

## Today I Manifest....

(Notice five things that you can see and write them down.)

| | |
|---|---|
| #1 | |
| #2 | |
| #3 | |
| #4 | |
| #5 | |

# Evening Routine

### This went well today

### 5 Things I am proud of

#1 _____
#2 _____
#3 _____
#4 _____
#5 _____

### This made me feel happy

### My thoughts about today

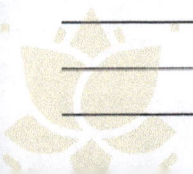

_____
_____
_____
_____
_____
_____
_____
_____
_____
_____

# Morning Routine

Date: _____

## Today's Positive Affirmation

## Today's Personal Goal          (Write down what you want to achieve for yourself today.)

_____

_____

## Today's Intention          (Write down how you want this day to be.)

## 5 Things I am grateful for

#1 _____
#2 _____
#3 _____
#4 _____
#5 _____

## Today I Manifest....          (Notice five things that you can see and write them down.)

| #1 |
| #2 |
| #3 |
| #4 |
| #5 |

# Evening Routine

## This went well today

## 5 Things I am proud of

#1 _____

#2 _____

#3 _____

#4 _____

#5 _____

## This made me feel happy

## My thoughts about today

_____

_____

_____

_____

_____

_____

_____

_____

_____

_____

"You Are A Creator...

✦

That Includes Your Thoughts!

# Morning Routine

Date: _____

## Today's Positive Affirmation

```
┌──────────────────────────────────────────────────────┐
│                                                        │
│                                                        │
│                                                        │
│                                                        │
└──────────────────────────────────────────────────────┘
```

## Today's Personal Goal

(Write down what you want to achieve for yourself today.)

_____

_____

## Today's Intention

(Write down how you want this day to be.)

```
┌──────────────────────────────────────────────────────┐
│                                                        │
│                                                        │
│                                                        │
│                                                        │
└──────────────────────────────────────────────────────┘
```

## 5 Things I am grateful for

#1 _____

#2 _____

#3 _____

#4 _____

#5 _____

## Today I Manifest....

(Notice five things that you can see and write them down.)

#1 _____

#2 _____

#3 _____

#4 _____

#5 _____

# Evening Routine

This went well today

5 Things I am proud of

#1

#2

#3

#4

#5

This made me feel happy

My thoughts about today

# Morning Routine

Date: _____

## Today's Positive Affirmation

```
┌─────────────────────────────────────────────────────┐
│                                                     │
│                                                     │
│                                                     │
│                                                     │
└─────────────────────────────────────────────────────┘
```

## Today's Personal Goal

(Write down what you want to achieve for yourself today.)

_____

_____

## Today's Intention

(Write down how you want this day to be.)

```
┌─────────────────────────────────────────────────────┐
│                                                     │
│                                                     │
│                                                     │
└─────────────────────────────────────────────────────┘
```

## 5 Things I am grateful for

#1 _____
#2 _____
#3 _____
#4 _____
#5 _____

## Today I Manifest....

(Notice five things that you can see and write them down.)

| #1 | |
|----|----|
| #2 | |
| #3 | |
| #4 | |
| #5 | |

# Evening Routine

## This went well today

## 5 Things I am proud of

#1

#2

#3

#4

#5

## This made me feel happy

## My thoughts about today

# Morning Routine

Date: _____

## Today's Positive Affirmation

```


```

## Today's Personal Goal

(Write down what you want to achieve for yourself today.)

_____

_____

## Today's Intention

(Write down how you want this day to be.)

```


```

## 5 Things I am grateful for

#1 _____
#2 _____
#3 _____
#4 _____
#5 _____

## Today I Manifest....

(Notice five things that you can see and write them down.)

#1 _____
#2 _____
#3 _____
#4 _____
#5 _____

# Evening Routine

This went well today

5 Things I am proud of

#1

#2

#3

#4

#5

This made me feel happy

My thoughts about today

Color Me......

# Morning Routine

Date: _____

## Today's Positive Affirmation

```
[                                                            ]
```

## Today's Personal Goal

(Write down what you want to achieve for yourself today.)

_____

_____

## Today's Intention

(Write down how you want this day to be.)

```
[                                                            ]
```

## 5 Things I am grateful for

#1 _____
#2 _____
#3 _____
#4 _____
#5 _____

## Today I Manifest....

(Notice five things that you can see and write them down.)

| | |
|---|---|
| #1 | |
| #2 | |
| #3 | |
| #4 | |
| #5 | |

# Evening Routine

## This went well today

## 5 Things I am proud of

#1

#2

#3

#4

#5

## This made me feel happy

## My thoughts about today

# Morning Routine

Date: _____

## Today's Positive Affirmation

```
[                                                            ]
```

## Today's Personal Goal

(Write down what you want to achieve for yourself today.)

_____

_____

## Today's Intention

(Write down how you want this day to be.)

```
[                                                            ]
```

## 5 Things I am grateful for

#1 _____
#2 _____
#3 _____
#4 _____
#5 _____

## Today I Manifest....

(Notice five things that you can see and write them down.)

| | |
|---|---|
| #1 | |
| #2 | |
| #3 | |
| #4 | |
| #5 | |

# Evening Routine

This went well today

5 Things I am proud of

#1

#2

#3

#4

#5

This made me feel happy

My thoughts about today

MANIFESTATION is
a graceful dance
between a PURE heart
and centered
INTENTIONS

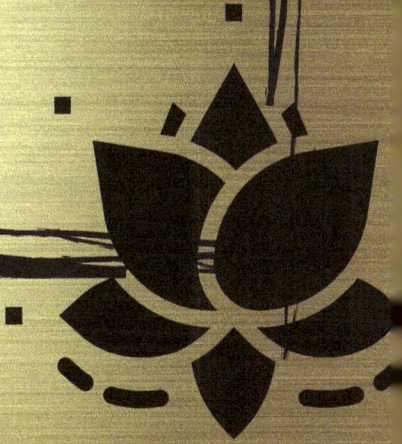

# Morning Routine

Date: _____

## Today's Positive Affirmation

## Today's Personal Goal

(Write down what you want to achieve for yourself today.)

_____

_____

## Today's Intention

(Write down how you want this day to be.)

## 5 Things I am grateful for

#1 _____

#2 _____

#3 _____

#4 _____

#5 _____

## Today I Manifest....

(Notice five things that you can see and write them down.)

#1

#2

#3

#4

#5

# Evening Routine

## This went well today

## 5 Things I am proud of

#1 _____

#2 _____

#3 _____

#4 _____

#5 _____

## This made me feel happy

## My thoughts about today

_____

_____

_____

_____

_____

_____

_____

_____

_____

_____

# Morning Routine

Date: _____

## Today's Positive Affirmation

> [blank box]

## Today's Personal Goal

(Write down what you want to achieve for yourself today.)

_____

_____

## Today's Intention

(Write down how you want this day to be.)

> [blank box]

## 5 Things I am grateful for

#1 _____
#2 _____
#3 _____
#4 _____
#5 _____

## Today I Manifest....

(Notice five things that you can see and write them down.)

#1 _____
#2 _____
#3 _____
#4 _____
#5 _____

# Evening Routine

This went well today

---

5 Things I am proud of

#1 _____

#2 _____

#3 _____

#4 _____

#5 _____

This made me feel happy

---

My thoughts about today

_____
_____
_____
_____
_____
_____
_____
_____
_____
_____
_____

# Morning Routine

Date: _____

## Today's Positive Affirmation

|  |
|  |

## Today's Personal Goal

(Write down what you want to achieve for yourself today.)

_____

_____

## Today's Intention

(Write down how you want this day to be.)

|  |
|  |

## 5 Things I am grateful for

#1 _____
#2 _____
#3 _____
#4 _____
#5 _____

## Today I Manifest....

(Notice five things that you can see and write them down.)

| #1 |
| #2 |
| #3 |
| #4 |
| #5 |

# Evening Routine

This went well today

5 Things I am proud of

#1

#2

#3

#4

#5

This made me feel happy

My thoughts about today

I Manifest The Things I Want By Believing In Their Existence!

# Morning Routine

Date: _____

## Today's Positive Affirmation

```
[                                                      ]
```

## Today's Personal Goal

(Write down what you want to achieve for yourself today.)

_____

_____

## Today's Intention

(Write down how you want this day to be.)

```
[                                                      ]
```

## 5 Things I am grateful for

| | |
|---|---|
| #1 | |
| #2 | |
| #3 | |
| #4 | |
| #5 | |

## Today I Manifest....

(Notice five things that you can see and write them down.)

| | |
|---|---|
| #1 | |
| #2 | |
| #3 | |
| #4 | |
| #5 | |

# Evening Routine

## This went well today

## 5 Things I am proud of

#1 _____

#2 _____

#3 _____

#4 _____

#5 _____

## This made me feel happy

## My thoughts about today

_____

_____

_____

_____

_____

_____

_____

_____

_____

_____

# Morning Routine

Date: _____

## Today's Positive Affirmation

```
[                                                              ]
```

## Today's Personal Goal

(Write down what you want to achieve for yourself today.)

_____
_____

## Today's Intention

(Write down how you want this day to be.)

```
[                                                              ]
```

## 5 Things I am grateful for

#1 _____
#2 _____
#3 _____
#4 _____
#5 _____

## Today I Manifest....

(Notice five things that you can see and write them down.)

| #1 | |
|----|----|
| #2 | |
| #3 | |
| #4 | |
| #5 | |

# Evening Routine

## This went well today

## 5 Things I am proud of

#1

#2

#3

#4

#5

## This made me feel happy

## My thoughts about today

# Morning Routine

Date: _____

## Today's Positive Affirmation

```



```

## Today's Personal Goal

(Write down what you want to achieve for yourself today.)

_____

_____

## Today's Intention

(Write down how you want this day to be.)

```



```

## 5 Things I am grateful for

#1 _____
#2 _____
#3 _____
#4 _____
#5 _____

## Today I Manifest....

(Notice five things that you can see and write them down.)

| #1 | |
|----|--|
| #2 | |
| #3 | |
| #4 | |
| #5 | |

# Evening Routine

## This went well today

## 5 Things I am proud of

#1

#2

#3

#4

#5

## This made me feel happy

## My thoughts about today

# Morning Routine

Date: _____

## Today's Positive Affirmation

```
┌─────────────────────────────────────────────┐
│                                             │
│                                             │
│                                             │
│                                             │
└─────────────────────────────────────────────┘
```

## Today's Personal Goal

(Write down what you want to achieve for yourself today.)

_____

_____

## Today's Intention

(Write down how you want this day to be.)

```
┌─────────────────────────────────────────────┐
│                                             │
│                                             │
│                                             │
│                                             │
└─────────────────────────────────────────────┘
```

## 5 Things I am grateful for

#1 _____

#2 _____

#3 _____

#4 _____

#5 _____

## Today I Manifest....

(Notice five things that you can see and write them down.)

| | |
|---|---|
| #1 | |
| #2 | |
| #3 | |
| #4 | |
| #5 | |

# Evening Routine

## This went well today

## 5 Things I am proud of

#1

#2

#3

#4

#5

## This made me feel happy

## My thoughts about today

# Reflection

Date: _____

Keep

Manifesting

Thau

Shxt

www.ingramcontent.com/pod-product-compliance
Lightning Source LLC
Chambersburg PA
CBHW070638150426
42811CB00050B/380